capitol fiction
by Marcellus Nealy

Tokyo Poetry Journal Subscriptions available via our website
(credit card, Paypal, bank transfer, or international postal money order
sent to address below).

¥1500/issue or ¥2500/year for individuals, ¥2500/issue or ¥3500/year for
institutions.

Make bank transfers to: Japan Post Bank
 (Account Name: Johnson Jeffrey Richard, Bank Code 10020,
Branch# 008, Account# 24951451).

www.topojo.com

social media
    facebook.com/tokyopoetryjournal
    soundcloud.com/youtube-topojo
    Instagram: @tokyopoetry
    X: @PoetryTokyo

ISBN: 978-1-957704-13-5

Capitol: the building that houses state legislature,

Capitōlium: the ancient Roman temple of Jupiter Optimus Maximus

Fiction: something that has been imagined, feigned, or fabricated; an imaginary thing or event presented for the purpose of argument or entertainment

"When you're young, you look at television and think, there's a conspiracy. The networks have conspired to dumb us down. But when you get a little older, you realize that's not true. The networks are in business to give people exactly what they want."

Steve Jobs

"Satire is a sort of glass, wherein beholders do generally discover everybody's face but their own."

Jonathan Swift

prologue

At the time of this writing, 23 years had passed since the world was stunned by one of history's most infamous acts of terror. The memory of it still haunts my thoughts.

On September 11th, 2001, I was flying from Miami to Tokyo. I can't recall the exact moment I heard the news, but I remember the overwhelming disbelief I felt. I also remember that I cried. I cried not just for the lives lost but for the dark depth of humanity's cruelty. What other sentient creature on Earth or in the stars could inflict such suffering and pain on each other?

The buzzword dominating the media was terror, much like it had been years earlier when I was a student during the first Gulf War. I remember walking through the halls of my American university when the news broke.

"We have gone to war."

The announcement on the television screens that lined the halls was met with a burst of abhorrent cheers from students shouting "Kick their ass!" and "USA! USA!"

The site and sound of it sickened me.

While they were celebrating I could only think about the doom that waited for anyone in the path of a tank or a missile. I mourned alone as the crowd chanted themselves into a frenzy. They were idiotic, young, and naive about the cost of war. Conflict is the invention of those in power, while ordinary people suffer and die, often with very little understanding of why.

Of course, there is always more than one telling of a story, and victims exist on all sides. No mother, regardless of nationality or faith, would fail to weep for a child lost to a war they may not have chosen.

capitol fiction

prelude

thoughts
stewed
social brews
plans upon
the hill
secrets kept
in smugness
snug
dumbness
statistical
data
acceptable
limits
of collateral
loss
and sacrifice
between
ham and
cheese
chuckling
bread
crumbed
crumpled
double chins
the motion
of our fate
begins.

part one

blistering
sun
on
65th
and
scoville
rancid
foam of
chicken bones
thrown
against the backdrop
of
a
long lost
tribe
high on
depressants
zombified
slow to dust
adrift in
brick
steel
color coded
cell blocks.
"help me
get
the
hell
out
of here!
somebody, anybody!"

what we need is
a negligible resource
eager disenfranchised
desperate in their decay and
starving.
line them up to the shave,
then stand them under the banner
symbol spangled star
for us to control.
they will be
the hands that hold
the bayonet,
the bullets
the bow,
they will be
the bludgeoning fist
the deadly blow
the feet that crunch
upon the bones
the bringers of our gold.

setting ball
beloved flame
across the amber sea,
five times a day
they call to he who is
protector of the land
amir drove fuzzy diced
through dust
and danced
to broken beats
and foreign well-wishers
in dining room
suburban oases
Where he would turn to hear
whistling strippers
searing loam
frightening speed
noncombatants
exchanging vows
veiled reflection
pristine gowns
a vision he would see
but never foresaw
as he practiced
his western
movie star guffaw

on scoville
the illhill gangsters
were making moves
the hood
as it was understood
was their place
their square
desolate
block of land
brick city outlaws
proud in stupidity
defiant against their place
impropriety for them
was outdated shoes
ill moded gear
and punk bitches
who they freely bent
over the table of fate
to blast
unlubricated
nonlugubrious
in the ass.

shuffle in the ruffle
the war room was ready
to lay its plan,
iron lads to show their holy
pristine white clean
to the network legions
monsoons of mogul minions
the word was terror
terror
terror
and plenty of it
anywhere the hour could strike
nowhere in all of the rolling hills
and plains of awarica
will we be safe
orange!? hell!
fiery red!
top level alert
sound the alarm
give them reason to fear,
give them reason to run,
edge of panic
stacked with a random act of utter
defile
on the evergreen
squeaky clean
heart of our great land
acceptable losses
for the new manifest
calling us to our foothold
and forever
freeing our lips
from the backsides
of oil slick slicksters
tricksters to whom we sold
part of awarica's soul

amir
was getting up in years
and always thinking
about california
about being a real action arnold
sweeping women in spastic swoons
brad
blade wielding weapon of
destruction wesley.
california
where one-line-locks are keyed
by handsome dudes
and blond bosomed jewels
who giggle out wishes
and lascivious whims
california
where the pop plush opulence
of song would suckle his ears
"amir, amir"
away the nights in fine attire,
ballroom dancing
and daydream fire
along the dusty dessert
unpaved portent of road

yo man!
i needs to get out of here.
cain't take this shit no more.
slanging is all we do,
ambition is lost to the wayside
with folks glocking folks
and getting lips for pipe hits.
i did this shit for the loot yo,
to feed my fams yo,
break from the roach motel,
you know what i'm sayin
a brother's gotta do
what he can
but check it,
i cain't be up in this mug
thugging for the rest of my life, dog.
i gots to get some skills,
get me a education,
maybe go to college,
rub elbows with the man
up in one of them plush offices
sippin on cognac and shit
i needs me a house
i can buy with legitimate ends,
have some kids and a dog,
barbecues on the lawn.
yo man, check it,
mikey dead,
ruff rider dead,
g money dead,
skillet dead,
big ben dead,
so i gots to step off
before i'm put in my cof
six feet deep for real

confirmation
secret routes
covert movement
blazing arabian suns.
planes to the target
promised spectacle
to rival none
blind them enough
demand revenge.
eight years prior
plausibility
they tried to no avail
now to hear the wail of
women lost to their
suffocating husbands,
time strapped
limbs strewn
homes blown back
into sand

we will rain rubble
upon their heathen ears
we will ring the wave
shock of horror
centripetal
to drum
to drum
round resounding
drum of war.

allah wakbar!
allah wakbar!

amir
sang his praises to heaven
the acceptance letter
had finally come
ucla
his father worked
years in toil
bent and scarred
for a chance
at a western education
at making a place
in the modern world

amir
pranced in circles
around the table
mom clapping
to the oud and rebab
tunes that billowed
from the old radio

amir
to be on the air soon
bound for sunny patios
and lively disco rooms
where the faceless friends
in wish-to-be places
would wave him down
to dance.

the recruiter stopped him in the mall
shiny shoed crew cut in bright white hat
crispy neat and looking proud.
he asked a name a place an age
as situation or circumstance or fate
would have it
he was from the same part of scoville
only 63 instead of 65,
the reds he said and
talked about things malik would know
but left them vague
to the years that passed
since supposedly he had got out
how the marines had made him a man
gave him skills to deal
world travel and fat checks from uncle sam
no chump change rinky dink
the real deal complete with 4 years
graduation university style
love for our great land
out of the ghetto
to send money to his moms
he flipped the stiff placard
eagle rose embossed in his fingers
wondered about germany japan.
learning to shoot.
hand to hand
mechanical know how
no more life on bull's-eye for an 8th
he could stand with the few
be with the proud
and escape the wraith wrung
legions
on exotic soils
far away from
the scoville scorn

dark down deep
in the earth hole
where the lights blipped and
satellite shots flickered
the big brass and
their wide bellied cohorts
plotted
the course
the line
the time
the places
the bureau was warning,
some were getting wise,
plausible deniability
the shield to cloak them
from reflection of their crimes.
8 years ago failed
flawed impenetrable
deflecting cases
to obscure investigation
two to be the projectile
third for effect
fourth bound
shot down
hidden from the news.
we will have
our place in the sand
we will plant
a flag in the hands
of everyone
with a camel
or a towel
we will pump
until we reach the bleed
to feed our fat relations

amir
veered by a friend's house
to boast of his good fortune
he sandpipered
around the room
then puffed
on a fake cigar
his friends
made fun of him
to cover
their casual envy
brochure photos
lush terrain
faces of people
diversely smiling
arab kid
backpack
shoulder slung.
polo shirt
blue jeaned
below 75 degrees
of fahrenheit
sun

yo the cops! run!
confusion
discombobulating
breathless
havening
just last week rock steady shot a man
for trying to steal his loot
then out of spite
he took that niggas' boots
damn fools
look at what they did
accessory to homicide
he ran
ran like runny grits
ran like greyhounds rolling out of state
ran a rickety and wild run
ran like carl when he was in his prime
ran like a fool that don lost his mind.
he ran off his ass
like hounds on his trail
like thoughts out of focus
like shrub for election
cutting through alley ways
jumping over fences
dead in the wrong
but running anyway,
running for lost hope
running away from himself
away from the dope they tossed
when the sirens flashed
howling call
to cause the scatter
cops on foot
slurs and sweat
catching up with night sticks
broken bones

bullets thrown
he ran

damn,
they were at his house
asking his moms
questions,
what kind of questions
how many questions
it was rock steady
who pulled the trigger
who pulled the blood
who pulled that poor fool's life
through a hole
in his god damned skull

part two

commander and chieftain
slipped away from the white house
to play golf and go fishing.
the nation
was on auto pilot
mispronounced
misspelled
misspoken
misled
he knew nothing about oppression
or education
knew nothing about the poor
people of the appalachians
their opossum feasts and fancy
eats of mountain oysters
fresh off the pig
he had never been on foreign soil
never had a passport
never looked into the eyes
of anyone from a different space
shit kickin beer guzzling
rodeo wanna be
mediocre on his own accord
good graces
paternal intervention
steered into the jagged boulders
way right of the shore
bible thumping god fearing
christian
still he knew
even if no one told him
the country was not his
florida rigged
tens of thousands to the poles
turned away as criminals
who never so much as sampled

a supermarket grape
he knew about the machines
in cahoots with the fox
terror was rising
rising in the hexagon
rising with dusty clouds of debris
rolling though the avenues
into the eyes of the people.
even as he was reading
piggly wiggly
green peas and spam
to his booger eating constituency

amir was at the market
choosing nuts and honey
for deserts so nice
they would almost
make him hate
to leave home
were it not for
the blasting heat
heart of the inferno
melting the weak skinned
business men
shuffled around the city
in air-conditioned cars
almost time for prayer
for amir to rush home
five times a day the call
from the muezzins in the minarets
rolling over the city in song
deep reverence
spiritual reminder
that they were bonded
in brotherhood
under the honorable and most high
he who had seen it fit
for amir to travel
over rocky waters
to deep blue swimming pools
and cool tropical drinks
forbidden to imbibe
but imbibe he would
and hope for forgiveness
god is great
the chant
the mantra
the call
across the lands

bowed upon knees
before the lord of abraham
amir
missing the motions
eyes on tight skirts
bikinied walkers
unstoned
freely roaming
already at the university
shuffling about
with handfuls of knowledge
between the halls
in libraries
on tree lined lawns
grass beneath his knees
under a just right sun.

you are nothing
do you understand me!
you are scum!
you are lower than scum!
if you were on fire
you would not be worth
the piss it took to put you out.
when i speak to you
you respond
sir yes sir
is that clear?
"sir! yes sir!"
maybe you've been sucking
on your mama's teat too long
i want to hear you strong
i want to hear you proud.
i will make men out of you
if i have to beat each and every
one of you maggots myself.
do i make myself clear
"sir, yes sir!"
he knew what he was getting into
before he signed his name
weeks of humiliation
down low in the mud
they gave him a riffle
they gave him a gun
they cut his dreads
until all that was left
was the skin of his head
mornings they worked him
muscles discipline
one of the few the proud
drill time in black boots marching
melting off the baby fat
the 18 years of scoville grime

"i don't know what you been told..."
the chant the mantra
prostrate in pushups
becoming a steel eyed
hero of awarica.
clear and free
from the hood
he would make good on his dreams
with every bullet he shot
with every quip he took
with every peace of grit
with every sir yes sir
he could see himself getting
stronger and closer to his big willie office
far away from the yellows
the greens
the blues
and the reds

n e w
pork city
fresh baked
b a g e l s
w a f t i n g
as the sleep
crumbs fell
from eyes
early birds
a n d
ball street
first risers
w o r k i n g
f o r c e
financial
heart of
the nation
a l r e a d y
m a k i n g
their way
i n t o
buildings
fingers on
the button
terminals
a l i g h t
email away
s o r t e d
j u n k e d
f i l e d
rich folk
in front of
the glass
with their
morning cup
l o o k i n g

out   over
the   rows
of   concrete
steel   and
taxi   cabs
as the nose
of   those
7   6   7   s
o p e n e d
w i n d o w s
t   o
m a d n e s s
m a y h e m
the   end   of
the   world
no   midday
q u o t a s
no long wait
till   lunch
no   quick
check   of
p e r s o n a l
s   i   t   e   s
no   phone
calls   home
no business
m e e t i n g s
no   shuffle
b u s t l e
e n d l e s s
r u s t l e
of   paper
no   hard
f r o z e
b u s i n e s s
p   o   s   e

no   poker
face in the
money race
the   day
would   be
s u d d e n l y
cut   short
the   office
c l o s e d
f o r e v e r
due to forces
b e y o n d
a l m o s t
a n y o n e ' s
c o n t r o l

the ovaline crew
rallied the boys a proper
retaliation
only a few were in the loop
secret society puppeteers
high theatrical fashion
as shocked as anyone would be
the country under attack!
"terror, terror,
goddamn those terrorists!
[cue card]
this is an act of war! call the
president"
[cue card]
shrub was in the middle of green
peas and spam
when the whisper came
allowing him to pause in the story
just long enough
for dramatic effect
he went on to the part
about trains and boxes and foxes
and in the dark
and could you would you in the
dark ...
in the midst of the panic
shock screaming streaming tears
of those at the bottom
of the building
the frantic char broiled
careening of those at the top
a second winged wonder
made a beeline
spectacular smack
splattering spattering
dicing explosion.

oh my god!!!!!!!!!
oh my goooooood!!!!!!!!!!!!!!!!!!!!!!!!
from the fiftieth floor they dove
taking their chances with gravity
against the hopelessness of
surviving the flames

again the whisper
in the ears of shrub
"...say...
i do...
i do like green peas and spam
...i would eat them in the dark..."

despite his scholarly reading
he was perturbed nervous shocked
lost for words or action or reaction
without a blink to moisten
his protruding eyes
he looked long into nowhere
as if he had missed something
or had a secret to conceal
the cart had been tipped
they had a target
they found a way
to bring him in
don't go to work
we got your back
old buddies
industry insiders
given a pass
to the richest
well sprung spring in the world

"...thank you thank you ham i am!"

amir had one week
before school began
he decided to take a flight
to npc so that he could
get a glimpse of the big bacon
nervous at the airport
long lines of people
passports flashed
shuffling past grimacing guards
with machine guns
off on the air
away from the dessert heat
away from the sand
to the land
where hip hop was born
and music flowed in the street
like never ending dreams
he wanted to see it all
do it all
experience it all...

spectacular shows on lawdway
street performers
corned beef rubens
washed down with a coke

"next!"

back to reality he shuffled
forward to the counter
handed his newly printed passport
smiled and told the clerk
he was off to awarica...

"gate 52a. next!"

on board the plane fidgeting
sitting longer than he ever had
prayer time came and went
came and went
god would surely understand the
position he was in
cheap flights take longer
with layovers and changes
a thousand years would pass
before he reached npc.

finally landed
hustled off
immigration
more scowls
looking down at passports
asking why he was in awarica
why he had traveled so far
for business, pleasure, subterfuge
amir told them he was a student
university in california
his english impeccable
from hours of practice
and imitating hollywood
his accent was there
but otherwise undetectable
as the guard looked
into his smiling eyes and said
welcome to awarica.

baggage claim
everything was strange
weird new wonderful
other worldly
free furious and fascinating

so many types of people
some round plump
fat on thin legs
reaching for bags
children running
early morning tired eyed
travelers rolling
customs check
opening bags
waving people by
waving amir onward
to his connecting flight where soon
he would be able to see
the spot where the snicks
play basketball
where blue bote
does its jazzy howl
across the avenues
that great sprawling oasis
central bark
mimes square
the imperial slate building
the world take center
and the statue of lippity
reaching up her great big torch
bare armed to the open skies.

two hours
another machine
bags rechecked
boarding pass passed
into the hull
of an aluminum giant
the bullet nosed bird
off and away
long away

far over the east
over new pork
spiraling buzzing
zooming into the heart
of the city seas

"allah wakbar!!"

the incredulous screams

"we will see heaven and be bathed
by a thousand beauties we will be
wrapped in the arms of god
allah wakbar!
we will see the dragon demon
spawn of hell fall
our families rewarded.
allah wakbar
we will be
the martyred
heroes of our day ..."

"no no no no no not today please
i am wanting to live, wanting to
see!"

and saw he did right up close just
outside the small window next
to his seat the big twin scaling
skyscrapers scraping against the
outside of the plane scraping away
the flesh of the people
row by row until
he was stripped clean
of his awarican dream

all right men this is it
the president has officially declared a war on terrorism.
get your gear together cause in three days at 06:00 hrs
we are going to offtanistan
where we will kick some contraban towel-head ass.

"so soon?" he thought
what about college and his big willie office
all the places the recruiter promised
he would get to see
he never said anything about offtanistan
he mentioned germany, japan, korea but never
offtanistan.
hell he thought he would make it through
the years of his commitment
just long enough to get a skill
get a job, get an education
never have to fight in a war
three days had passed too quickly
he and his platoon were on the march
...something about marines
being the first to arrive
the first to kick ass.
they were the few the proud
the scared out of their god damned minds
18 19 20 21 22 23 years old
niggers from the ghetto
spicks from the barrio
chinks from china town
camel jockeys from convenient stores
red neck sons of bitches
...all of them in their own way
escaping life
looking for funds
for a career
for hope

for regular meals
for self-discipline
for freedom
from a life at the bars

"we will get in and get out.
we will strike hard and fast.
we will subdue the enemy
with little or none of our casualties.
your country needs you
your president needs you
the world needs
you we must protect our freedom
must protect the future of our children
you are the heroes of the day
you are marines..."

he was pumped excited scared
he had never been in a war of course
but felt it was probably no different
than fire fights in scoville
where bullets whipped past his ears
on more than one occasion,
he had seen blood, guts spilled
bodies crawling in the streets
he had heard the pow powerful kick
straighten a boy backward
down roads where cars spat bullets
on unsuspecting fools
he told himself he survived it
and that it would be no different
that he had bigger guns this time
although he had never taken
another human life
he had seen it enough times
on tv and in the streets

to know how
fuck it.
he was going to war
in the dessert of offtanistan,
might as well get the shit out of the way
so he could get on with his big willie dream

the transport was long,
there was no comfort for the fighting man
some guys were scared
they had heard horror stories
from the early 90's
gas and chemicals
melting eyes and peeling skin
after effects lingering for years
missing limbs
desert death

the sergeant told him
this war was different
they had more precise weapons
they could hit a mouse
on the forest floor
without rustling the trees
they could burn a snake
right out of its hole
without disturbing the sand.
sergeant was there in the last war
he said it was a hoax
cooked up by spiteful folks
who have no respect
for the sacrifices
a soldier makes
like the sacrifice
malik almost made
when his vehicle

was ambushed
instant as a flash grenade
he regretted enlisting
slinging in scoville
he begged god for forgiveness
begged to be saved
the black hood
the beatings
the messages
he was forced to speak
the hunger
dried blood
caked under his nose
the weak wave of hopelessness
that rose inside of him
the gunfire
the running
the yelling
after endless confinement
the sweet sound of english
blinding sunlight
helicopter blades
on a stretcher
of a miracle
alive
free
away

oh! why have they done this
why have you taken my boy
amir! amir
allah why
what have we done
we are people with simple dreams
he was a nice boy
a kind boy
a good soul
too good to burn
inside that awful plane
too good to suffer
didn't they check to see
if they were killing
their own people
didn't they care
that innocents would fry
with their infidels
amir had no hate in his heart
only infatuation and curiosity
his only hate was
for those those who would kill
in the name of allah
terrorists
who bomb and shoot
infidels and innocents
children and soldiers
all in piles of blood and bone
under the endless tears of god

part three

.

"get me anything
that will link this to sodom
anything" said shrub
as he tried not
to trip over his strings...
daddy dearest
giver of all i have
and all i know
i will bring you his head
for what he tried
i will place the spike
on your front law
for you to enjoy
as the flies eat
away the meat

terror

they hit the world take center
they brought it down
to the rumbling ground
they struck at the
heart of our precious land
they defiled our soil

terror

sound the alarm

terror

boil the blood
of the awarican people

terror

the hexagon
the world take center
anthrax in the mail
orange
red
rampage

terror

who knows
where they will strike
what school yard
what puppy farm
what dal-mart
hell
even the amish aren't safe
to secure the security
we must go to war
stop these terrorists
before they can strike again
the axis of evil is in motion
a coalition of the indebted
will march into caves
and barren wastelands
to eradicate the problem

terror

the world will know
terrorism the buzz
we will be the busters
to stop it

in the infirmary
there were boxes from his local perish
cakes, candies and well wishes
the good reverend goodfoot
had taken up a collection
when he heard the boy had been captured
lucky for him
it was just a few bruised ribs
a fractured nose
and a lot of broken skin
lucky for him
he made it out alive
to promises of an easier life
the war for him was over
sergeant would personally see to it
that he made it to college
he whispered in his ear
about a practice blond set aside
so he could get the grip right
the days came and went
but he was still in the desert
still in the hung low humidity
of the hot sun.
everyday folks flown in
blown up badly damaged
bleeding and bandaged
no legs no arms
no arms and legs
monstrously burned
howling in the night
calling for morphine
afraid to die
the flat line
the endless sleep
inside the desperate
desert heat.

...it didn't matter the cost
in money or lives
the snake hole
was a lot smaller
than they thought
the mice on the forest floor
couldn't be seen
without clearing the trees
two years had passed
with the passing rubble
memories began to fade
they needed to strike
strike with more fear
dark evidence
satellite pix
strange shapes
building clusters
maybe bombs
boney scare
predict the fall
economy! culture! jobs!
mosque by a manger
stranger danger
from bearded men
and women in hijab
back pack bombs
arctic parkas
sewn into suicide vests
with 17 virgins
to call them all
to their senses
call them all
to our side
we are going
on a country fry

democratic process
will not stop
our freedom
this is war
roll in the tanks
smite them where they breed
with the help of the havemores
and the television feed
we will
demonize
dehumanize
fustigate
and purge that scourge
to the fires of living hell
the sudan
can wait
the congo
can wait
those people are too hungry
to fight for very long
let them wear
themselves out
our business is here

malik was on a base in the middle east
fixing machines and supporting
just as he was told
in and out they said
but they were still there
even though they promised
the war was over
the contraban were dead
they were still combing the mountains
looking for benny and the jets
who for all we knew
had shaved their beards
and were chilling
on a beach in thailand.
he felt gypped
by his own pride,
he was a marine
he survived
god was on his side

shock hit when the news came
another location
another war
"didn't we kick their asses
when i was 9
why do we have to go back"

malik swore he had no luck
then thought twice
as he was still breathing
off they went into the thick
the first ones landing
the last ones standing

"no more sick duty
we need men

able bodied
strong arms
you can walk
you can drive,
you can carry a gun
you can fight"

"sir yes sir"

"now move out"

wild eyed fear
fumbled misfire
they had blown up
the wrong building
the head of a little girl
rolled to his feet
even on the worst
days in scoville
screaming mothers
never spat on him

red wedding dress
lipless grin
the mind melding stench
of people charred
inside a stripped out
stronghold

never never
in all his days of slinging rocks
did he watch people crawl
into the scope
to be blown into darkness
without a weapon to be seen
no hint of mass oblivion

traces of murder machines
combatants hiding in buildings
crouching low on rooftops
shooting riffles
and rocket launchers
instead of anthrax,
nuclear mustard sarin vx
laden things
where were the barrels
labeled hoboken and springfield
where were little boy and fat man
labeled awerica or bust

malik ran through the ruble

"i am a marine, i am a marine
though i walk through the valley of the shadows
i fear no evil cause
i am the baddest mother fucker in the valley"

the chant the mantra
he ran past a hand
in the middle of the road
past heads that dozed
between snarling bullets
deeper growling than scoville
he ran
ran behind burnt vehicles
right back into enemy arms
no merciful fists or gracious kicks
no one to greet him
to take him to his cell
just a jagged edge
from around a blind spot
to hug him tightly
and carry him away

"awaricans are
safer
sodom has been taken
down
we have him in
a hole
he is no longer
a threat
many awarican's
have lost their lives
sacrificed much
for their country
we are saddened
by loss
uplifted
by the new age
it brings
terrorism
must end
we must be
the ones
to stop it"

amir's family had
little time to grieve
they needed to escape
with only enough for one
to morroco or egypt
anywhere without doom
before the bombs blew
amir's brother flew
to carry on the family name
his father and mother
aunt and uncle
"residential stronghold"
of unknown terrorists
militia men chosen
to be the snake in the hole,
the mice in the field
how he wept
and was done with war
he hated awarica
he hated terrorists
he hated shrub
he hated sodom
he hated himself
for being
the last one
alive

in   scoville
a   n   d
in   ilack
d e s p i t e
what   was
officially
s a i d ,
w   a   r
continued
rock steady
was   jailed
t   h   e   n
s h a n k e d
inretaliation
a c r o s s
the   land
a   butcher
p a c k e d
his   riffle
for   a
s h o o t i n g
s p r e e
high school
m e t a l
detectors
alert   the
living dead
d r o w s y
d r u g g e d
lousy   in
all   the
s c o v i l l e
multicolored
multiracial
multiethnic
broke   ass

broken
down busted
ghettos   of
a w a r i c a

shrub   and
his   secret
b   a   n   d
s c o t - f r e e
with   never
a   son   to
boot   camp
d a u g h t e r
to the mud
all   for
f r e e d o m s
r   i   p   p   e   d
w r a n g l e d
and wrested
in our name

s o m e b o d y
ring   that
d   u   d   e
i   n
outerspace
so he can
come   by
bless   this
p   l   a   c   e
and   save
us   again
from   our
m   o   s   t
terrible sins

epilogue

let me go now
fore it really
gets   bad
fore my door's
kicked   in
and my place
is full of gas
leave   me
my   skin
no   atomic
c r a c k s
c h e m i c a l
b u r n s
peeling   on
my   back
i can feel the
ground shake
16   hooves
pounding   to
this   place
let me away
before   they
a r r i v e
with my teeth
u n c h a r r e d
and   my
balls   unfried

biography

Marcellus Nealy is a native of Cleveland, Ohio, USA, and a co-editor as well as contributing author of Umoja: ToPoJo Excursions – Black Diaspora Edition. Since 1992, he has been a prominent figure in Tokyo's poetry scene, known for his unique blend of improvised free verse and live musical performances. His work often explores themes such as challenging societal norms, seeking spiritual enlightenment, and celebrating both art and life.

Professionally, Marcellus wears many hats. He serves as an associate professor at a renowned university in Tokyo and lends his voice as a narrator for Japan's public broadcaster, NHK. Additionally, he works as a ringside announcer for MMA events and is a supporting member of the Japanese pop band DREAMS COME TRUE.

www.ingramcontent.com/pod-product-compliance
Lightning Source LLC
Chambersburg PA
CBHW051241120626
46547CB00014B/1745